# REALITY,
## a potential cure for poor behavior


by

## Gary and Gaydra McCallister

# DEDICATION

To our parents who introduced us to reality.

# ACKNOWLEDGEMENTS

It is impossible to identify and recognize all the many people who have contributed the ideas in this book.  We make no claim that these ideas are original with us.  This book is simply an attempt to clarify in writing what we have found useful in raising and teaching children for over fifty years. We have raised four children to independent adulthood and taught hundreds of others, both children and adults. The brotherhood and sisterhood of parents and teachers have contributed to our knowledge and we hope this book may contribute to someone else.

# TABLE OF CONTENTS


| Chapter | Title | Page |
|---|---|---|
| | Acknowledgements | 3 |
| | Introduction to reality | 5 |
| 1 | What people need | 14 |
| 2 | Principles of reality | 23 |
| 3 | Six steps to living in reality | 37 |
| 4 | The dialogue of reality | 45 |
| 5 | Epilogue | 51 |
| | About the Authors | 56 |
| | Other Books by Gary McCallister | 57 |

# INTRODUCTION - REALITY AND BEHAVIOR

*I'm not crazy about reality, but it's still the*
*only place to get a decent meal.*
*Groucho Marx*

## Overview

The reason for writing this book is to provide a method of helping children learn to conduct themselves in a way that is compatible with reality.  Fortunately, the same methods can also be useful in helping some adults with behavior problems. Many people of all ages who misbehave in some way have never learned how to live peacefully with reality. Accepting reality can have a great effect on helping people change and find greater happiness and success in life.

The first part of this book addresses the issues of behavior in the real world.  It isn't that the real world is so hard to understand.  It's that not everyone has spent enough time thinking about the real world.

This isn't necessarily a character flaw.  The real world is often difficult, demanding, multiple faceted, and filled with distractions.  Many children exist in extremely difficult circumstances and basically live from crisis to crisis. Even an idyllic childhood can seem demanding and overstimulating to children. Under such conditions they may have little opportunity to develop skills in problem solving, planning, and judgement.

In addition, the modern world is filled with distractions such as television, cell phones, video games, school, social events, and extra-curricular activities.  It is difficult to think clearly during irregularly occurring snatches of time with many ideas competing for attention. This is the condition of most adults in the world and responsibilities and demands on their time and energy.

That is why this book deals with teaching people with behavior problems how to successfully deal with reality.  It does not address severe misbehavior such as mental illness or addiction.  However, it is a valuable method of helping people become well adapted to society and overcome common self-defeating behaviors.

## Why should you read this book?

Jacob was flunking out of High School and there seemed to be nothing his teachers could do about it. Tests and personal conversation showed him to be exceptionally bright and articulate although quiet. He wasn't shy when you spoke to him or called on him in class. The problem was he just didn't turn in his outside work and assignments.

Molly was from a seemingly good home that was better off economically. She was one of the more fashionable girls and always dressed in current styles. She was popular and had a good group of friends. So why had she now been picked up, twice, for shoplifting?

Mrs. Giles was at her wits end. Her husband was going to be late to work again this morning. He stayed up late playing video games and then refused to get out of bed until the last minute in the mornings. She wished he understood it wasn't only his business. He'd already lost two jobs for being habitually later.  What was she supposed to do but nag?

Jim controlled his irritation with difficulty. The lid was off the toothpaste again and the toothpaste tube was all crumpled and distorted instead of being squeezed neatly and efficiently from the bottom. Why couldn't his wife take the trouble to do this when she knew it upset him so much. "Susan!" he yelled.

## Self-destructive behavior

Many people struggle with self-destructive behavior, or at least behavior that causes them and others distress. In the last example I don't know if Jim or Susan has the problem. Maybe they both do. But in each case people seem to be making choices that are harmful to themselves and causing concern for others.

Interestingly, many people resist changing their behaviors when their harmful behavior is pointed out to them. Parents, spouses, teachers and even official authorities are often at a loss about how to help these individuals to better regulate their lives. Pointing out their faults and reminding them sometimes turns into power struggles, nagging, and endless arguments and unhappiness.

People often make mistakes and bad choices, but seldom because they are bad people.  Most people who are irritating or misbehaving are simply trying to fulfill their needs. Sometimes people choose inappropriate behaviors for fulfilling their needs because they are disconnected from reality in some way.  People are often not even aware of what needs they are trying to fulfill.  Sometimes they are just unaware of reality. Other times they may be aware of reality, and simply decide to ignore it. Neither choice leads to a very happy or productive life.

Much of the poor behavior a parent, teacher, coworker, employer, or employee must deal with is not truly "bad" in a moral sense.  Occasional, workplace violence gets a lot of press but, thankfully, it is rare.  Most poor behavior is along the lines of disruption of the environment, thoughtlessness of other people, or simple self-defeating behavior.

Irresponsibility, carelessness, and disrespect for others, are behaviors that do not help children, or adults, live full and successful lives. Not turning in your homework, not getting up on time, or being chronically late are self-destructive habits.  Making excuses, being unreliable, or blaming others are not the ways to make friends and influence people.

Respecting property, privacy, and feelings make for a happier family, classroom, business environment, or for that matter a happier life.  Even mild antisocial behavior such as fighting, stealing, staying out past curfew, swearing and chewing tobacco can be changed, since they are often an attempt to fulfill some need.

Those who deal with people making poor choices and who must watch them harm themselves are often frustrated and don't know what to do. In many instances, such as parents or teachers, they are even somewhat responsible for helping individuals make better choices, but they do not know how to achieve their goal.

Often, in our attempts to help, and not seeing results from one activity, we try something new. Perhaps we first try to reason with the person. If that seems to not help, we criticize. If there is no change, we nag, get angry, cry, and then reason again. Our frustration mounts and, I can assure you, so does the frustration of the person you are trying to help. Constantly shifting approaches do not engender a feeling of security in the part of the one being dealt with. And security is one of the basic needs of humans.

**Staying calm**

What if there was a simple and consistent method of approaching people and aiding them to make beneficial changes in their life? What if there were a method for staying calm, consistent and effective when dealing with behavioral issues? What if there was a method that often gave good long-lasting results in making people's lives better.? What if this same method could also help you, the parent/teacher/employer/whatever stay calm and feel good about your attempts?

What if I told you this book provides such a method? Would you read it? Because it does.

**Who are we to tell you what to do?**

This book grew out of the combined efforts of my wife and I to raise our children and to earn our living as teachers. Actually, the need to raise our children led to the need to earn a living.  That's why both my wife and I were schoolteachers.  The need for a job is one of the first things a person learns about reality by having children.

Anyway, we have both experienced the reality of having raised our own children and of trying to teach something to yours.  If we combine our histories with reality, and share what we have learned, we hope to save as many people as possible from having to learn the realities of life the hard way.

There may be no easy way to learn the realities of life. But we all need to learn the realities someway and learn how to negotiate our own realities in a way that fulfills our needs without harming others.  That is, we're trying to spare you our experiences, not your own.

The principles shared in this book are based on ideas that others have discovered and taught in many ways, under various names, in the past.  We don't claim to have discovered anything about reality that isn't already known.  My wife and I searched out methods of teaching our children about reality when we discovered that not all people recognize reality when they see it. This is often a problem with children as they mature.  Sometimes it is a problem for mature children.

## Our personal needs

We adopted the methods found in this book when we realized that they worked consistently in most instances. These ideas are simple, consistent, effective, and helped us from having to reinvent the wheel, stumble and fall, despair, and yell as frequently as we might have.  Perhaps more importantly they helped us avoid anger and punishment. They helped us raise four children and never be turned over to family services. Not even once.

These methods also aided us in dealing with classrooms full of children and young adults for many years.  My wife taught elementary school while I taught at a university dealing mostly with young adults. Not all students, or adults, are equally adjusted to reality, and this missing ingredient often caused them to engage in self-defeating behavior. While we could not deal with every student, or with serious mental health issues, we did have a method of dealing with less minor, but still damaging and disruptive behaviors.

While this set of principles and ideas are simple, they do require some practice to implement.  I guess it is like a hammer or a pair of pliers.  They aren't very complicated but perform best when used by one who has had a little practice. Don't get us wrong.  Hammers and pliers should not be used when dealing with people and reality unless it is absolutely clear that they are the proper tools.  We have found this is hardly ever the case.

## What will you get from reading this book?

Have you ever ordered an ice cream sundae when you are determined to lose weight? You are either denying or ignoring reality at that moment. Or you were denying or ignoring reality at the moment you decided to lose weight. You can decide which.

Have you ever bought something you knew you couldn't afford? Perhaps you have put off doing something you knew had to be done sooner or later. Too much television? We all have our moments when we deny or ignore reality.

For most mature adults they are rare, transient, recognized, and accepted, or at least tolerated. However, not everyone is a mature adult, even many mature adults. And children are especially prone to be out of touch with reality. Their experience with reality has been limited simply by the fact that they are children and haven't lived with reality for very long.

The goal for this book is to teach a very specific set of six steps that can help a person deal better with reality. However, the steps sometimes seem counterintuitive and may be a little hard to apply unless one understands the reasons for each step.

Consequently, there will first be a chapter on what people need in their lives and how they sometimes go about trying to meet those needs. This is not an exhausting, psychoanalytic approach to all possible needs and causes. It is simply an understanding of what most of us are trying to achieve in our daily lives.

This will be followed by a chapter detailing the principles on which the steps presented later are based. If you understand the principles, you will be more willing to try and adopt the steps as they are formulated and have more faith in their consistency. The principles are the important part of the method of teaching reality. The steps and the dialogue which will be explained later are the shortcut version of the principles.

The principles of this six-step approach also help explain the dialogue that one can use to help another identify their approach to reality and make better decisions. The actual dialogue is of little use if there is not a relationship of some kind between the parties involved. That relationship will be developed through these principles.

There will be a chapter in which a specific dialogue, in a specific sequence, is introduced that in most instances will take a person through the steps of recognizing and dealing with reality. It can be reapplied as frequently as need, thus providing a calm and consistent response to poor decisions on the part of another.

## The job of behavior modification

What is the best tool?  This question is, of course, nonsensical.  The answer to this question depends on what the job is.  A hammer is not the most useful tool for removing a screw from a board.  It might get the job done, but it will require extra effort and may have serious consequences for the board.

Just like any toolbox, when the job is "changing a person's behavior", there are multiple tools available: threat, force, pleading, punishing, hollering, teaching, explaining, persuading, and so forth.  Most of us use all these tools at one time or another.  Threat and force are quite popular. Hollering is one of many people's favorites.  Blowing off steam doesn't accomplish much in changing behavior, but, at times, it can make the person hollering feel better.

There are times when we use too many tools at once. We often use first one tool, and then another, and then another, as we grow more frustrated.  This is counter-productive because the people we are trying to help don't know what to expect from us from time to time.  They become as confused as we are; and, for a lot of us, that can be pretty confused.  Maybe the first rule of reality should be that we must be in better shape than the ones we are trying to help.

Progress occurs best when there is consistent, proper, and skillful use of the appropriate tool.  When "changing behavior" is the job, the work goes better when there is consistency in the message and method to be used.  We have found consistency to be a valued, though often elusive, goal.

## What's in it for me?

As a parent, teacher or someone who is concerned with another who is making poor choices, the task is to somehow convince them to alter their behavior. So, this method is a behavior modification tool. Like all tasks, there may be many tools available and part of the responsibility of the workman is to select the appropriate tool.

If someone you know and care about is trying to satisfy their needs in unrealistic ways, it will help them if they find realistic ways of satisfying their needs.  That's the theory in a nutshell.  People are not always fully aware that they are avoiding reality because they are not being realistic. However, if you are being unrealistic in your behavior and expectations, you are, by definition, avoiding reality.

So, the job is to help them learn to enjoy dealing with reality. We don't say it will be easy. We just maintain it will be worth it.

Some of the advantages for applying the concepts in this book are that they are:
- simple to learn,
- consistent to use,
- effective,
- and they avoid the use of anger and punishment.

Their application might even allow you to remain friends with someone after they face reality.

## How can you get the most of this book?

The dialogue for helping someone change their approach to reality is found in chapter 4. It's not a secret.

However, unless you understand the reasons for each step in the dialogue you may not think it sounds reasonable, you may find it difficult to apply to a conversation, and you may not be able to use it effectively

This is not a long book and if you will read from start to finish, I think you will find the best results from attempting to use this approach with your children, students, or employees.

*A man said to the universe:*
*"Sir, I exist!"*
*"However," replied the universe,*
*"The fact has not created in me*
*A sense of obligation."*
*- Stephen Crane -*

# CHAPTER 1

## What People Need

*I don't like work... but I like what is in work - the chance to find yourself. Your own reality - for yourself, not for others - which no other man can ever know.*
*- Joseph Conrad -*

Everyone needs something. Personally, I need a new guitar.  My wife maintains that is just a "want".  She simply doesn't realize how much I need it!  She says the reality is that we can't always get what we want.  I say, if we try, sometimes we might get what we need.  I think the Rolling Stones said that first.

If we assume that people behave in ways to satisfy their needs, we probably ought to have some idea about what human needs are.   Of course, we also must distinguish between wants and needs.  It can get confusing if you need something, so you can do something else that you only want to do.

Anyway, people who are desperately hungry would probably steal for food if they had the chance.  I know I would.  In fact, my mother always said that I did.  People who are afraid often act unpredictably, like cornered animals. You just never know if they will run or attack.

So, let's review a few of the need's humans try to fulfill through their behaviors.  They will be used to clarify some of the techniques that we will introduce later in the book.

## Human needs

Every human has basic physical needs to stay alive. There are times when even these basic needs may be lacking and can cause behavioral problems. However, these physical needs don't always have to be lacking to cause problems if there is just a reason to fear that these needs may be unreliable. The fear engendered by the loss of work leads to lack of confidence in fulfilling future needs and can cause behavior to change. So, lets first identify the physical needs humans have.

## Physical Needs

Of course, people really need food, air, water, clothing, and shelter.  These are the basic requirements for life.  It's the amount of each of these things that is open to debate.  Some need more guitars than others.  It may even be that there are folks who shouldn't receive any more food, water, air and such.  That remains an open debate.

It seems to me that many children blame their parents for what they did, completely losing sight of the fact that they were fed, clothed, and sheltered to grow up to complain. It is nice if parents can do more than that but doing less than that is not responsible parenting. Society and culture may make it seem as if much more is required such as music lessons, athletics and perfect psychological behavior. But those things are optional.

However, as soon as the life requirements mentioned are met, humans seem to immediately desire something more.  The need for these additional desires is sometimes debated, and different behavioral scientists may have slightly different lists and priorities.  That's to be expected of behavioral scientists who sometimes have different concepts of reality.

But you are probably not a behavioral scientist, and I am for sure not one.  For the purposes of this book we will lump all these additional basic needs as "security" and "identity".

## Emotional Needs

These two needs, security and identify, have a great deal of very real effect on a person's behavior.  Insecure people often behave as if they are insecure.  And people with multiple identities often don't know who they really are, or which person they are at any given moment.

Fear. People who are insecure or confused are most often afraid, and fear always greatly changes a person's behavior. When people are comfortable and secure, they almost always behave differently than when they feel threatened and endangered.  There doesn't even need to be a real danger but can only be a perceived insecurity.  People hollering at you can seem intimidating even when they are only calling you to the telephone.

Also, because we see our behavior as normal and unthreatening, does not mean that others see our behavior the same way.  You may want to go to Back-to-School-Night because you see that as the behavior of a caring and loving parent.  Your child may see your going to Back-to-School-Night as very threatening.  Hey, the teacher might see you as very threatening.

Frightened people, like frightened animals, often behave impulsively and in unpredictable ways.  One can never tell what a startled wife might do if you jump out and scare her.  At least so I am told.  Children of divorce sometimes act out in antisocial ways.  This is a function of insecurity and a fear of the unknown.  People may feel insecure and fearful because of circumstances, failures, criticism, threat, anxiety, or even exhaustion.

<u>Identity.</u> Once people are accustomed to their situations, and less fearful, they begin to form identities for themselves. This sounds simple but can get complicated. For example, my identity may be that I am a decent guitar player. This works until I am sitting in the company of a good guitar player.  Since the identity of being a good guitar player is no longer available in that circumstance, I need to invent a new personal identity for that moment.  Who knows what it will be?  Probably not even me.

Self-identity is not the same as perceived identity. Often people we may see as being very capable are very unconfident themselves. I may see myself as the strong, silent type. However, my family might find the concept humorous.  How we see others may not be at all how they see themselves.  How others see us may not be at all like we see ourselves.

The process of forming a personal identity goes on over a lifetime and is based on an unidentifiable number of influences. Young children seldom have a clear perception of

16

their own identity because creating an identity is partly a function of higher-level thinking. Early childhood seldom involves higher level thinking.

During early childhood, a person's job is to experience, remember, recall, repeat, and modify our behavior; not necessarily identify who they are.  The acquisition of individual personal qualities is important for our physical survival, but they are relatively simple mental exercises. Learning the meaning of words and learning how to control our bodies are essential skills, but they do not require the creation of many sub-categories or fine distinctions.

Self-identity is partly a function, in children at least, of the development of higher-level thinking.  As our mental abilities mature, we begin to use our knowledge of the world to form categories and to classify objects and people.  This allows us to see similarities in various groups. The categories we form may be taught to us by adults.  Friends, families, teachers, and even public media influence our thoughts and decisions. Of course, we all formulate some of our own categories based on individual experiences.

The act of putting things into categories where the elements are not actually identical, but similar, is a powerful mental action that we tend to take for granted.   We tend to see things that are not identical by some aspect that we think they share or not.

For example, we learn to identify a dog when we see it even though there are a lot of different kinds of dogs.  In fact, we learn to tell dogs from cats though most people can't describe in words the difference between the two.

Habit makes us think these categories are obvious. However, they are not obvious as is evidenced by the dog/cat delineation.  In fact, not all languages share similar categories.  I am told some languages in the Pacific have no word for tree, but every individual tree has a name.  This ability to order things into similar and dissimilar categories is the foundation for creating human language.

However, people establish many categories of their own making based upon their own unique experiences, as well as those categories that may be taught through their culture.

This causes each of us to see the world quite differently than others do. Children seldom perceive their parents in the same light that the parents perceive themselves. And teachers have unique perspectives about their students than the student may have about themselves.

## Two major identities

One of the major categories that young children begin to understand at an early age is one concerning their own abilities.  They begin to see themselves as "successes" or as "failures".  These are broad categories of how they identify themselves and becomes a part of their reality.

How they identify themselves in this category begins around six years of age for most children.  It ends around the age of ninety-three, so I am told!  Interestingly, we are mostly unaware of the process as we experience it, just as we are unaware of most of our behaviors as we do them.

The two categories are seldom complete categories. Most children recognize that they are successes at one thing but less successful at others. This success/failure identity is added to over time and is an individual experience.  The resulting self-image doesn't necessarily have anything to do with their actual experiences or how others see them. Where they fit in this category depends on their own experiences. For example, if one shares experiences with older siblings, they may feel a failure in activities by comparison.  In fact, they can be performing perfectly adequately for their age.

The various experiences of youth reinforce themselves over time.   These self-identified categories may have little to do with actual achievement or the experiences of an individual as seen from an observers' perspective.  What is important about the self-described identity is that the people who see themselves in one of these two ways tend to diverge over time and get further and further apart in performance.  These self-identities often become stronger and stronger until the identify they have created may be very difficult to change.

For example, those who fail to grasp early math concepts well tend to continue to struggle in math until they stop doing math at all.  Success in early math leads to more success in later math, and the two groups grow disparately apart.  The same applies to other areas of our lives.  Early exposure and success in music tends to lead to later success in music.  Early and rich language experience tends to lead to greater fluency.

## Behavior problems

Behavior problems frequently develop in people who have developed failure identities.  Failure identities are often accompanied by insecurities.  Remember that security is one of the basic emotional needs of humans, after their living needs have been satisfied, so failure sets them up for a double whammy of behavioral issues. Insecurity and fear are the twin children of poor behavior.

The reality is that almost no one needs to be insecure, afraid, or feel like a failure.  Almost everyone has the capacity to be successful at something, and most likely many things.  The definition of success is a difficult concept, but most people can live a successful life.  However, if they see themselves in an unreal fashion, they may behave in ways that ignore reality, or ignore the real consequences of their actions.

## Categories of poor behavior

Children who grow up feeling like failures tend to fall into two categories, or even to bounce back and forth between the two categories.  Since their real world feels threatening to them because of security reasons, or because they feel incapable of coping with their real world, they may tend to:

- 1) deny reality or
- 2) ignore reality.

People who deny reality often retreat into fantasy worlds, and their behavior may seem extreme to others because they are acting out a fantasy existence.  These children may get lost in books, movies, video games, art, music, or other narrow interests that allow them to escape reality.

Alternately, their behavior may become irresponsible to real world obligations because they are lost in their dreams. Not tending to real responsibilities does not increase one's happiness.

The other tendency in people who perceive themselves as failures is to ignore reality.  Such people may be perfectly aware of their behaviors, but they just ignore the consequences as if the consequences don't really exist. When grounded, they sneak out.  When denied, they steal. Of course, not all negative consequences can be denied, and they end up with worse and worse consequences being imposed on them.  This further strengthens their failure identity.

In addition, denying and ignoring reality can be dangerous.  Defying gravity, excessive speeds, spending money extravagantly, experimenting with drugs, violence, reading novels in class, and arguing with the First Sergeant can have very real consequences which, if ignored, can prove painful or deadly.

## The problem with reality

The problem with reality is that it is real.  Our circumstances are not mere figments of our imaginations. Regardless of whether we like our circumstances, we still live in them.  Some realities truly are threatening and difficult. Many realities are beyond our control.  Regardless, people must find some way to live in their reality the best way they can.

You may be in an accident, through no fault of your own, and lose a limb.  That is very painful and learning to live a normal life afterward is extremely difficult.  However, the reality is that you don't have that limb.  You will still find it necessary to make your bed, fix your food, dress yourself, and make a living.

Children may live in abusive homes.  It may be very difficult for them to apply themselves to school, do homework, or find significance in academic subjects when their real world seems dangerous and is falling apart. Nonetheless, their best bet for escaping such an environment, their real world, is further schooling.  It would be best if they felt secure in their home. But they must stay in contact with what is real and consider the consequences of their own behavior towards their goal of escape.

A married couple may be unhappy together.  It may be very difficult for them to handle all the problems of a family: finances, behaviors, desires, and responsibilities.  However, the reality is that divorce leaves both people less economically well off, lonelier, more frightened, and with feelings of failure.  This does not even take into consideration the proven harm done to their children.

My wife's father lived with us a for a few years before he died.  He was frail, weak, and had some dementia.  He wanted to sleep all the time and would have literally stayed in bed twenty-four hours a day if allowed.  We knew this was bad for his health, but it was also very difficult for my wife to deal with and still have a quality life.

So, we explained to him, many times, that everyone has certain responsibilities and obligations. His was to get up at the same time each morning, clean up for the day with help if needed, and make his bed.  He could go to bed at a specified time.  In between, he could do what he pleased. Even three-year-old children can do these things.

## The concept of reality

Reality is the concept that gave this book its title. Insisting on reality in a quiet way while applying pressure to be connected to reality and the consequences of behavior is one of the secrets to success in changing behavior.  This can be surprisingly difficult at times, because the ones who are supposedly in charge may have their own struggles with staying in touch with reality.

However, there are principles that can be applied to help the parent, teacher, or friend help someone else who is escaping or ignoring reality.

The next chapter will begin to explore those principles.  Later we will provide steps you can take to follow those principles as well as a dialogue to help you put the principles into action.

> *Today's scientists have substituted mathematics*
> *for experiments, and they wander off through*
> *equation after equation, and eventually build*
> *a structure which has no relation to reality.*
> *- Nikola Tesla -*

# CHAPTER 2
## Principles of Reality

*You can avoid reality, but you cannot avoid*
*the consequences of avoiding reality.*
*- Ayn Rand -*

It is difficult to change long-developed and long-held concepts, especially when they have developed unconsciously and from your own direct experiences. In fact, it is often impossible for a person to even recognize that what they believe is not reality. It has been their reality for a long time. Asking them to jettison what they have learned through experience is a frightening and insecure activity that they will not do easily.

Consequently, in this chapter we wish to lay out nine principles that we believe to be true about what is required to change a person's behavior who is causing problems or being self-destructive or self-defeating in some way.

The following principles are not uniquely applied to reality. They matter when applied to fiction also. The difference is that, when used in fiction, it doesn't matter so much if they work or not. If they don't work, it doesn't matter. Actually, in fiction, it doesn't matter if they do work. It's fiction. However, these principles do apply and matter when applied to reality.

There are basic behaviors and tendencies of people that influence all kinds of human interaction. If you want to have positive influence with someone, these principles apply. In all honesty, if you don't use these principles you will still influence people. It's just that the influence may not be as good or as effective at helping them face reality. Even if you don't follow the dialogue at the end of this book, you will find these principles key to dealing with people, normal people, who have lost touch with reality in little ways.

We are aware that you cannot remember nine abstract ideas for very long. We can't either. That is why we have written them down. We refer to them often ourselves to see if we are approaching a task in the best way. However, it is important to review them first so that when we come to simpler procedures you will understand the principle behind the set of simpler steps and dialogue.

## Nine principles

Here are the nine principles for dealing with reality. We will present them first simply as bullet points and then devote some explanation to each principle in the next section.

- People must feel cared for and secure.
- People must know you care.
- Be subjective and personal.
- Deal only with present behavior.
- Each person is responsible for their own behavior.
- Focus on behavior, not feelings.
- Accept no excuses.
- Catch them doing something good.
- When and how to change is up to the individual.

## What do these things mean?

1. People must be cared for and feel secure

It is difficult to concentrate on draining the swamp when you are up to your neck in alligators. When people are in severe trouble or feeling threatened, they are probably not capable of logical discourse or reasoning.

In the police station is not the time to discuss issues such as "What were you thinking?" If the trouble is real, it would probably cause further harm trying to analyze the situation. What is needed at such a moment is safety and security.

Even when the troubles are not true dangers, but emotions are high, reason and logic are generally not persuasive or even heard. I always wonder how much of what coach's shout from the sidelines the players even hear. In fact, I know for a fact that instruction hollered at me, even in the huddle, are seldom understood. True behavioral change probably can't occur until a person feels safe, cared for, and secure.

Once the threat and fear are minimized, then one can proceed to discuss identity and better ways of interacting with real situations. It is often difficult to organize a safe place and situation for all concerned, but by doing the best you can you will maximize the opportunity to help someone.

2. People must know you care

If a stranger were to walk up to you on the street and tell you that your clothing was in poor style and inappropriate, you would probably be embarrassed and maybe even angry. However, I would not advise you to take your anger out on them in a physical way.  That would simply cause more, very real, problems.

By contrast, if I am about to head off to work and my wife looks me over and gives just the slightest frown, I am anxious to know what is wrong with how I'm dressed.  I pester her until she tells me specifically what is wrong, and I change.  Well, unless she orders me to change.  Then I probably won't, even if she is right.

Furthermore, there are people to whom I would never pay the slightest attention on matters of their opinion about me, or anyone, or anything else.  Yeah, you know who you are.  If I do not like or trust you, I am not likely to consider your opinion.

As a rule, people do not accept instruction from total strangers, people whom they lack respect for, or people they may perceive as enemies.  This holds true, even if they normally trust you but you bark orders at them.  Barked orders make them perceive you as the enemy.

It is probably beyond the scope of any book to tell you how to sincerely convince people that you care about them. Suffice it to say that you probably must begin by sincerely caring about them. What is true is that they must at least believe your good intentions towards them. That is your challenge before any dialogue can be undertaken of any kind.

3. Be subjective and personal

The counter point is that we do care about what our friends and family think.  This means that if people are comfortable with you and value your relationship you can have a positive influence on them.  That is, if you want to have influence, the people need to see that you care.  They must be comfortable in your presence.

There are many ways to make people feel that you care about them.  One way is to ask them about their lives, their desires, their difficulties.  If they think you truly understand their situation, they are more willing to listen to your opinions.  This is especially important for people who may see themselves as mostly a failure of some kind. Listening to them and understanding that some of their perceptions and reality may be exactly that, a reality.

But another way to establish a friendship is by talking with them about yourself, your desires, your difficulties.  Sometimes you can even effect a change in their behavior by asking them to make the change for you.  If the children are making noise and you have a headache, it is simple to ask them to be quieter just for you.  "Do it for me," sometimes works well, at least in the short run.

Authority and speaking down to people are seldom perceived as caring. Further, it is almost always suspected of ulterior motives benefitting the authority, not the person being counseled. Keep things personal.


4. Deal only with present behavior

This may be the most difficult thing to do on the list of principles. It sounds so simple yet one of the most difficult principles to live.  In fact, it is probably the most difficult task entirely, when dealing with other people.

It is human nature of almost everyone between the ages of two and one hundred and twelve to try to divert attention. It is often uncomfortable to be singled out in front of a group. Even positive attention is often uncomfortable, and we may attempt to dismiss it as quickly as possible.

When the attention is negative, we may feel even more desperate to divert blame. And if we can't divert blame, we will try and divert attention.  The ways of diverting attention and blame are many and may be subtle.  However, these attempts usually involve trying to divert attention to another:

- time,
- place,
- event, or
- person.

Children often try diverting blame to another person.  "He hit me first!"  Of course, this invites the inevitable "two wrongs don't make a right" discussion.  However, it often also leads the discussion off into why he hit first and what caused that which was caused by something else.  By then the discussion is no longer about hitting but has become a moral morass, and the parents are at their wits end to untangle the web of behavior.  Can you relate?

Adults are not immune from this behavior.  How many people blame their poor behavior on parents with whom they haven't lived for twenty years?  One son is an alcoholic because his father was an alcoholic.  His brother doesn't drink because his father was an alcoholic.  How many thieves stole because of their mothers, girlfriends, or their buddies?  It's funny how people never steal because they are thieves.

Here are some examples of how people excuse poor behavior by diverting attention:

"Back where we come from . . .." (Place)
"We do it the way we've always done it."  (Time)
"That's the way my father did it."  (Person and time)
"It was a dark and stormy night."  (Event)

Personally, I have tried to explain to my wife that I am absent minded because of my abusive childhood when we didn't have a television and all I had to do for entertainment was read.  She doesn't think that is any real reason for forgetting to put milk away after breakfast.

Humans frequently divert attention from their poor

behavior to their feelings.

"I don't feel like it."

"I gain weight in the winter because of the winter blahs that make me eat too much."

"I did it because I was under a lot of stress."

However, feelings are notoriously fickle.  If we wait until we "feel" like doing something, we may wait a very long time. And if our misbehavior affects others, our feelings about it may be of very little importance. We may feel like drinking and driving. Others may have strong feelings about your wanting to do so.

Because of this universal tendency to redirect attention, there are only two solutions that have any bearing on changing behavior.

- The present poor behavior and
- plans for the future.

These are the only things that can be profitably discussed. Reminiscing about ancient wrongs or rights, criticizing someone else's behavior, analyzing a series of events, and other such activities do not change the present reality and future consequences.

Everything except current behavior and plans for the future simply goes into an endless discussion of cause and effect.  Since every event has a cause, and another event causes the previous event, this solution is fruitless in changing behavior.

We are aware that this idea flies in the face of a lot of psychology which holds that people must discover the causes of their poor behaviors and feelings. But since initial causes cannot be changed, nor can the cause that caused the initial cause, these topics are useless in changing behavior.

Granted, there are some behaviors that may need such psychoanalysis.  But these cases dealing with serious issues should be handled by a professional.  For much of the common, everyday types of self-destructive behavior, the cause is not what's relevant.  Effective change can often be enacted simply by facing reality. The desire to escape or ignore reality can be very strong.

   5. People are responsible for their own behavior
One of the difficult lessons people must learn along the way to living is that we cannot change others.  People cannot force anyone to change.

   This applies to parent and child, employer and employee, teacher and student, dealers and addicts, cops and robbers, or ministers and congregants.  We cannot really change others.  The best we can do is change the way we relate to the other people.  Living successfully in reality requires a set of behaviors we can use to change how we relate to those around us.  When we change ourselves, others will change in response?

   This makes sense.  If we act in certain ways, other people react in certain ways.  If I walk up and slug you, you will very likely slug me back, unless I make it an awfully powerful blow to begin with.  On the other hand, if I hold the door for you, it is very likely you will hold the next door for me.

   This means we must give other people the power to change and place the responsibility of changing directly on them by helping them learn how to make that change.  It is their responsibility.

   Responsibility is difficult to accept sometimes and can be burdensome.  However, the reality is that everyone has responsibilities; and to act as if we don't make mistakes never makes for a good adjustment to reality.  By kindly and quietly insisting that the other person accepts responsibility, and then teaching them how to do so, is a great service to them.


   6. Focus on behavior, not feelings
Reality can certainly change our feelings. When I am injured, or someone is rude, I may feel sad or angry. A dark and stormy night can make me feel frightened. A hard day's work makes me feel tired. Watching food ads on television might make me feel hungry. Reality is irrefutably tied to our

feelings.

The problem with feelings is that they don't change reality. I may feel pain and feel like I want it to go away. It generally ignores our feelings. I may feel angry, but it will not change the other persons driving. It may well be true that you are sick, or old, or unhappy.  Hard circumstances don't make the reality of life go away.

If you have failed to pass the exam, it doesn't change your grade to say, "But I studied hard."  If you hit someone and injure them, it doesn't take away their pain, your responsibility because you lost your temper, or your legal consequences.

In fact, feelings are probably the least reliable way of getting anything done. If we wait until we feel like doing somethings, especially somethings we have a responsibility for, we may wait a very long time. Doing our homework when we feel more like it is a recipe for late, hasty homework and missed assignments. Cleaning our room when we feel like it generally leads to dirt and disorganization.


7. Never ask "why?"

Okay, maybe I was wrong. This might be the most difficult principle of them all. When people behave in ways we don't understand, we are perplexed.  We think, if we understood their behaviors, we can help them change better. Their behavior seems so far off from our perception that we simply can't comprehend what they are doing.

However, this assumption is simply not true. In fact, it is hardly important at all for you to understand why I do things. That simply satisfies your curiosity.  It is far more important for the person who has the behavior problem to understand that they have behaved as they do.

For example, I might understand that you stole something from me because you were hungry.  You have still broken the law, my trust, and I will still be deprived.  While your theft creates a behavior problem for me and how I will relate to your act, it does nothing to solve your behavior problem of stealing. My understanding will not be of any use to you in your efforts to be an honest upright person.

The problem with asking people why they are behaving in a certain way is that they will then tell you.  Generally, people love to talk about themselves. But what they tell you will be an excuse, not the real reason.  They will probably tell you something to direct attention and blame away from themselves.

Whatever they say in answer to the question "why" becomes an excuse.  Its purpose will be to deflect attention to someone, some place, or some other time.  So, you see, asking "Why?" invites excuses, and excuses are deflection of attention, not reasons. Therefore, there can be no excuses.

Excuses do not address what was done, what they are doing, or how to correct their behavior.  They invite you to change the subject to the excuse.

If a person has difficulty keeping promises because their father was an alcoholic, we do not have to find out why the father was an alcoholic. We do not even need to understand how his father's alcoholism causes the child to break promises.

Even if it is true that the father has caused the child's behavior, the child must still take responsibility for their behavior and find a way to correct it. Even if we determine that the father was an alcoholic, the person will have to figure out how to keep promises when they don't. Other descendants of alcoholics do keep promises. So can they. So, the unreliable person doesn't need to explore the effect of alcoholism on children.  The person needs to determine how to be more reliable.

If your daughter hits your son and you ask why, she will tell you it's because he did something to her.  You will then ask him why he did that, and he will tell you it was because of something she did.  You will then have to discover why she did what she did that made him do what he did that made her hit him.  The talk about the inappropriateness of hitting people is lost amidst the "whys".

But what if it is a "good" excuse?  Even good excuses don't change the reality of a situation.  If a person is on their way to a job interview but gets hit by a truck and wakes up the next day in the hospital, he will immediately call the business and explain that he didn't show for the interview because he was unconscious in the hospital.  He has a real, honest-to-goodness excuse.  However, the reality is he remains unemployed.

If I am a good person, I will feel sorry for your misfortune. I will think that you have been dealt a bad hand.  But my feelings and beliefs will not change the cards in the hand you have been dealt. You still don't have a job.

8. Catch them doing something good.

<u>We feel good when we do good, but not necessarily the other way around.</u> Consider the simple case of doing one's homework or maybe cleaning the garage.  If we say we will do it when we feel like it, it may be a very long time until it gets done.  I don't think I have ever felt like doing either one. And it will likely be done late and in a hurry.

On the other hand, when we jump in and complete tasks, we almost always feel good about our accomplishments.  Is the secret of getting a lot done, doing it to the best of our abilities, the simple solution to feeling good?  What about the time factor?  It takes a lot of time to do things well.

However, when people excel at something, they usually want to do more of it. The more they do of it the better they get.  The better they get the more quickly the accomplish the task and the time factor no longer exists. Further, the better they are at their task the more they want to do it, and thus accomplish a lot more.

> *That was a problem with my homework for the first eighteen years of my life.  My teachers just didn't know how to motivate me properly to want to do my homework.  (Notice how automatically and deftly I switched the responsibility to my teachers?)*

We often don't want to do the things that we feel inadequate at.  So, we put these things off and then do them in a hurry.  Our haste almost guarantees that they won't be done well.  We don't take pride in doing things poorly and, therefore, don't want to do them.  It can be a vicious cycle, or a benevolent cycle.  Teaching people to excel can certainly be a great blessing to them.

This is the reason for only talking about either present behavior or future plans. Behaving better, even for the

*I once attended a lecture on Biological Illustration by Dr. Lee F. Braithwaite at Brigham Young University.  The Professor asked the students how long they thought he spent on a particular illustration.  They all guessed several hours.  Since he logged his time on the back of his illustrations he was able to tell them the illustration took thirty hours.  They were impressed.*

*He went on to explain to the students that the secret of getting more done was to do everything you do as well as you possibly can.  Though that sounds counter-intuitive, his reasoning was this.  When you do the best you can, you are proud of your work and feel good about it.  When you feel good about something you want to do more of it.  When you do more of it you get better at it and then you feel even better about doing it.*

*I was more impressed than the students.  I knew the illustrations had been made for his lab manual in invertebrate zoology.  However, I also knew that his illustrations had been ruined thirty years earlier when a pipe broke and flooded his office.  He had made that illustration, or one similar on the same topic, twice.  Instead of quitting in despair, he had simply started over, with meticulous detail, to recreate all the illustrations for his book.  It must have felt good.*

moment, helps us to feel better momentarily. Planning to do better in the future is one sure way of doing and feeling better in the future.

9. When and how to do better is up to the person with the problem

If you are a parent, teacher, or work in some role as a counselor you are probably mature and at least somewhat successful at solving problems.  But in fact, it is almost always necessary that the person trying to help must be in better shape than the one they are helping. If you are an experienced problem solver and reality negotiator, several solutions to solve behavioral problems will seem obvious to you.

However, as surprising as it may seem, what you see as a problem, may not seem like a problem to the person who is being dealt with. When you say they shouldn't jump on the bed, they can see that obviously it upsets you that they are jumping on the bed. Having never dealt with the expense of broken beds or medical injuries, they may not see any problem at all. Their problem is "you are being concerned about it", therefore in their mind it is your problem. Therefore, their behavior is not their problem. Their problem is you.

On the other hand, the problem you perceive may seem very small and insignificant to them when compared to the entirety of their experience. Your concern with homework may seem insignificant to possibility of their father killing their mother some night in a drunken rage.

Your very excellent suggested solutions may not be something they are even willing to consider. Do your homework first thing after school may not match with their very real part-time job that they need to buy food.  Your solution may not fit their circumstance.  After all, you have never been in their exact circumstance dealing with nuances, restrictions, and expectations of which you cannot possibly be aware.

The bottom line is that "freedom is king".  People get to solve their problems, if they want to, the way they want to.

The government, or the councilor, may try to force them, but the individual will always trump the authority.  I learned this in the military when I discovered that Generals can order a hill to be taken.  But if the privates don't want to take the hill, it probably won't happen.

So how does one person "help" another?  The helper can help them think of consequences and whether they have considered those as real or not. The helper can help them identify a range of several possible solutions that they can choose from and try out. The helper can help them evaluate the possible consequences and applicability of each solution and encourage them to choose one to try. Making plans and setting goals are a necessary part of growing up and living responsibly in reality.

There are some general rules that relate to solving problems that can be suggested to someone grappling with reality.

- If there are no consequences, there is no change.
- People seldom change until they are uncomfortable in a way that is meaningful to them. They may be perfectly comfortable.
- If people do not see the consequence as bad, change will not happen.
- If people do not see the behavior as a problem they will not change.
- If we see that our behavior is a problem to others, we often think it is their problem to solve.
- if you identify the misbehavior, it is your problem, not theirs.

Let's say you walk in and find children jumping on the bed, and you say, "stop jumping on the bed".  If there is no consequence, they will not stop jumping. If the consequence doesn't matter to them, they will not stop jumping. If the children think their problem is you, they will just hide their jumping. If this persists their problem will be you, not the bed or the jumping.

The bottom line is that their freedom to choose whether to change, when to change and how to change is not up to you. All you can hope to do is encourage and guide their attempts to live in reality.

## What can I do?

When we were first introduced to these principles, we felt overwhelmed.  What else could we do to correct behavior?  These principles seemed to remove every option we thought we had for teaching and changing behavior.  You may also be feeling this way.

However, there are other powerful ways to deal with behavior issues, and we will begin to explore them now.  There are a series of steps one can go through which will help you help others face reality.  We will explain the steps to you in the next chapter.

> *"Reality is that which when you stop*
> *believing in it, still doesn't go away."*
> *- Philip K. Dick -*

*If you believe that feeling bad or worrying long enough
will change a past or future event, then you are
residing on another planet with a different reality system.*
*- William James -*

There are six necessary steps to follow when helping change another person's behavior.  These six steps put into practice the nine principles discussed in the last chapter. Remembering nine principles is difficult for me, and I suspect it is for most people.  However, we explained them as a foundation for understanding how the six steps work.

It's much easier for me to remember six sequential steps to take in helping others get in touch with reality.  I even use several of them on myself from time-to-time.  And the process is getting easier.  We have already reduced what you must remember from nine principles to six steps.  Here they are in a brief format. We will enlarge upon them following. We will further simply them in chapter 4.

- You must be personally involved with the person.
- The person must identify their own behavior.
- The person must identify the consequences of their behavior.
- The person must make a value judgement on the consequences.
- The person must make their own plan.
- The person must make a commitment to carry out their plan.

## Defining the steps

1. Be personally involved with the person

The student must see that you care.  Basically, caring is often spelled T-I-M-E.  You can show you care best by spending time with them and listening to them.  This, of course, relates to principles one and two. If you are dealing with your children and they do not feel that you listen, that may be the problem.

Trying to correct behavior at the same time the misbehavior happens is seldom effective because the person does not feel safe and secure, or like anyone cares about them.  That may be partly why they misbehaved in the first place.  Dealing with misbehaviors later also allows you the opportunity to demonstrate you care and your willingness to listen.

As mentioned previously, humans seldom respond well to instruction from strangers or people who they do not trust to be concerned with their own wellbeing. So, any person struggling with a poor relationship with reality needs to feel like you care about them if they are to listen to what you have to say. That's just reality.

2. Help the person identify their own behavior

The student must identify their own behaviors that are causing them problems.  This may seem insignificant but is extremely important for a variety of reasons.  We have discovered that people, namely our children, are extremely reluctant to identify their own misbehaviors.  They seem to intuitively understand that doing so presents a major problem for them.

The first and most obvious reason the person must identify their own misbehavior is to help them recognizes that their behavior is a problem.  What may seem an obvious problem for one person, may not really have crossed the mind of another. Children often see their behavior as just having fun and are puzzled by adult interference.

For example, small children jumping on a bed may not know that this is both potentially dangerous and damaging to the furniture.  In their minds, they are just having fun.  They don't pay medical bills or replace broken furniture.  Before instruction can begin, all people involved must recognize that the behavior is a problem.  That's just reality.

Of course, often people misbehave with a clear knowledge that there is a problem with their behavior but, for whatever reason, choose to misbehave anyway.  The reasons are many.  Perhaps the thrill of jumping is simply more fun than any vague perceived risk that they have not yet experienced.  Broken bones are hard to imagine until you have experienced one.  Perhaps they feel the reward is worth the risk. Then, perhaps they are addicted to the behavior.

In many instances, the person may not be able to think of a better way to behave.  Cutting class because their homework isn't done may be the only solution they can think of at the moment, even though they know it will result in further difficulties.  Not everyone is adept, skilled, and experienced in solving problems to the same degree.

By asking the person to identify their behavior, the parent or teacher can discover whether the person even understands that there is a problem. This helps the helper know how to proceed because misbehavior out of ignorance can be handled with teaching rather than penalty.

There is a second, powerful reason for having the individual identify their own behavior.  When a parent, teacher, or authority figure identifies the behavior for them, that behavior subtly becomes the problem of the one bringing it up, not the problem of the person misbehaving.

The person misbehaving assumes that if you are upset by their behavior, then you are the one needing to make changes.  They seem to think it is the teacher or parents' attitude that needs changing.  Not their behavior.

"Why are you jumping on the bed?" "I've told you not to jump on the bed!"  These statements or questions imply the person in charge has identified a problem that the person in charge has.   Parents don't like children jumping on their bed.  I just thought my parents were spoil sports.

Of course, we can make life uncomfortable for bed jumpers for a time by hollering or with punishment.  They may not want to be uncomfortable again, but mainly they have learned to "not get caught" jumping on the bed because parents don't like it.  Their activity is not a problem, but you seem to have a problem with it.

Thus, one way or another, a test of wills will start.  They will demand to know why they shouldn't jump on the bed.  They will justify why they should be able to jump on the bed.  They will tell you that their friends can jump on their beds.  They will tell you how many times they have jumped on the bed without consequence.  They will tell you that someone else jumped first.  And they may continue to jump on the bed when they think they won't be caught.

This scenario will not dramatically change if you substitute other common behavior problems such as not doing homework, lying, stealing, fighting, being rude and so forth.  We know because these things all happened to us, either when we were children, parents, or teachers.

When the person identifies the behavior that is causing them problems, you and they know that they understand what they have done.  They now own the mistake.  This is their connection to reality.  Regardless of the motives or causes of misbehavior, people must live with their behavior.  That is the reality of things.


3. Help the person identify the consequences of their behavior

If you are an adult in some position of authority over others, you are also probably a pretty good problem solver.  We can surmise that because you are still alive and in some position of authority.  Presumably, you are somewhat acquainted with reality, having survived to an older age and having been given some small authority in the world.

Surprisingly, not everyone in the world is very skilled at identifying consequences.  Children may be especially poor at the skill.  But even many adults seem to not understand that consequences follow behavior. Then again, many adults continue to live in a fantasy word or are aware of consequences but ignore them for short-term pleasures.

For example, someone might think, "I could get into trouble if I lie."  However, the idea of "trouble" might be extremely vague in their mind.  Trouble might be anything from a scolding, a spanking, or being sent to their room.

However, not everyone is equally affected by any of these forms of trouble. Being sent to one's room might even be a relief as it removes the person from a difficult situation.

Then, if people are caught up in the emotions of the moment, they might not be thinking ahead to consequences at all.  They may simply be desperate in their attempt to avoid the imminent discomfort of the moment. A person's definition of trouble may not include many difficulties that arise from poor behavior.

In either case, people often don't consider specific long-lasting consequences such as friends being disappointed in them or not wanting to play with them.  They may not have thought about the connection between the honesty and trust and the freedom and responsibility they desire. They may not be considering how the results their actions might affect businesses, families, communities, or even strangers.  They probably haven't even considered the law.

If we can help them to understand the consequences of certain behaviors, they can more completely decide whether the behaviors are worth keeping or not.  But until they have a clear picture of what "trouble" means, they obviously don't have a clear grasp of reality.

4. Help the person make a value judgement concerning the consequences of their behavior.

It may seem perfectly obvious to us that certain consequences are undesirable.  For example, when I, Gary, was a child, sending me to my room was not a significant punishment.  That's where my books and guitar were.

However odd it may seem, not all people experience consequences in the same way.  Taking away a privilege might be dire to one person and inconsequential to another. A cold, hungry, homeless person might even find a night in jail appealing.

If there are several possible consequences to a behavior, discussing the various outcomes may help them decide whether to continue with their behavior or not. Whatever the consequences are, the person misbehaving must regard them as undesirable before they will be motivated enough to behave differently.  People seldom change unless they are uncomfortable with the way they are.

There is another reason for helping people face reality. Since people are often behaving badly to satisfy a need, if they can identify activities that satisfies their need better, they may change their behavior. If they can identify a behavior that leads to a happier existence, they can change their minds from feeling as if they were a failure. If they can discover ways to accomplish their own goals they will feel more in control, successful, and confident.

5. Help the person plan for changing behavior.

One of the advantages of being married is that there is always someone to talk you down off the roof when you make mistakes.  The burden may fall unfairly between the two with one having to perform those duties more often than another.  But with two people discussing issues they can more easily identify a plan.

Mature people who are in touch with reality are often good plan makers and problem solvers.  They at least have a track record of having solved enough problems to have grown older.  Living usually involves making and following plans.  Stating that one is going to change does not in any way guarantee that one will.  Changing involves the formation of a plan.

Children are not necessarily good problem solvers, almost by definition.  But many, more-mature persons are often not skilled at making plans either.  In fact, this is one area where higher education proves useful. Higher education requires people to set long-term goals, as well as a series of sequential steps they must take toward reaching that goal. This training and activity are a powerful skill for living in reality. Many people learn to plan effectively without a college degree, but college is one good place to learn this approach.

In other words, some people may need to be taught how to make plans for solving problems.  It is very tempting, if you are a good plan-maker, to make plans that will solve the other person's behavior.  However, like owning the misbehavior is critical, owning the plan is also critical.

Parents often make plans for children that the child has no intention of following. Children may make plans their parents have no intention of allowing them to follow. Employers may the biggest plan maker for others. If the "other" do not like the plan or see the need for it, the business is in big trouble.

Not only do people want the freedom to make their own plans, they are also the only ones to recognize all the nuances and quirks of their own circumstances, habits, desires, and life that must be figured into it. It may seem perfectly reasonable to practice the piano every day right after school and then you can go play. The child may know intuitively that they are too tired, hungry, and distracted by the demands of the day to be effective.

6. Making a Commitment

We learned, when dealing with children at school, our own children, and even adults in the workplace, that when people say they will "try" to do something, or they "will see if they can", or even "probably will' do something, they most likely won't.  They just don't want to say no out loud and be confrontational or say yes and be held accountable.

There can be many reasons for hedging one's bets in making commitments.  A person may lack the resources to carry out the plan, such as obtaining a ride someplace.  They may need to consult with others for permission or rearrange a schedule because of other obligations.

Very often, however, these phrases are code words for, "I am going to wait and see if I get a better offer", or "I'm going to see what I feel like when the time comes".  If they are living their life by their feelings, or if they are not truly convinced the commitment is important, they will make similar weak commitments. It is amazing how powerful it is to insist on a commitment, either way.  When people verbally say, "Yes, I'll do it", they are far more likely to really do it.

Of course, if the plan is difficult to follow, they may need help in carrying out the plan.  If the person is not an experienced and successful planner, they may only be able to come up with a limited idea or plan. Gentle questioning can sometimes help them see more possibilities. A variety of solutions is more likely they are to find one that is acceptable to them.

One way of showing you care is by helping in needed situations.  But it is their plan and their responsibility to successfully complete it.  That's just reality.

## How do I do this?

Our problem has been in trying to remember and complete all six steps in a consistent manner.  While slightly better than nine principles, six steps can still be a little difficult to apply. We have discussed them here so you can see the significance of each step and why it is important that they be completed.

Thankfully, there is a simple dialogue that can be used in many situations. This dialogue has six steps, but all the explanation for each step is missing. Thus, the helping person simply must recall the dialogue, or series of questions to consistently apply these six steps.

Demonstrating that you sincerely care for the one you are trying to help is not included.  You're on your own on that.

With the theory for using reality in dealing with behavior explained, let's learn a specific dialogue for using the above six steps.  In the next section we will explain how to use a dialogue that will work to accomplish the six steps.  The steps may seem hard to remember or follow.  The dialogue provides concrete and specific structure to the steps.

*"If my hand slacken, I should rob God, since*
*He is the fullest good,*
*leaving a blank instead of violins.*
*God could not make Antonio*
*Stradivarius violins without Antonio."*
*- Mary Ann Evans, in (of Antonio Stradivarius)*

# CHAPTER 4
## The Dialogue of Reality

*Reality is what it is, not what you want it to be.*
*- Frank Zappa -*

We were tempted to call this the "Real Dialogue" but thought better of it.  It seemed grandiose, like all other dialogues were false.  However, the following dialogue contains all the elements contained in the prior discussion of reality. By asking the following six questions you will be fulfilling every one of the six steps identified previously, except establishing that you care about the person. That must be done in advance.

At first, the dialogue can be difficult to use. People are expert at deflection, and you will need to stubbornly concentrate on keeping to the subject.  But if you continue its use you will become better.  Your efforts will help the people around you to become more connected to reality.

With practice the dialogue becomes habitual, which is a benefit both to you as parent and leaders, and to the child or person you are trying to help face reality.  After a while, some of our children would look at our faces and mimic us before we could say anything.  "I know.  What are we doing?"

Above all, this tool works only when the person knows that you care about them and their well-being.  If you are satisfied that you've created this kind of condition, then the following dialogue accomplishes all six steps listed in the previous chapter.

**"What are you doing?"**
*(Step 1 - He identifies his own behavior.)*
This is all you have to say. It can be asked again and again until the person identifies their problematic behavior. If you feel silly asking the same thing again and again you can switch it around a little by saying something like, "Well, you were doing something.  What was it?"

If the student doesn't turn in his homework, and you ask about it, he might feign confusion.  He may also deflect by saying something innocuous like, "I'm going home."  You may have to follow up with other forms of the same question, such as, "Are you forgetting something?"  However, in no case should you say anything about his homework.  He or she knows and doesn't want you to know that they know.

Sometimes you will meet with stonewalling behavior.  He might refuse to give a meaningful answer.  Commonly, he might just shrug his shoulders and mutter, "I dunknow," or, "Nothing."  This can be followed up with, "Well, you are (were) doing something.  What was it?"  People can be very resistant in identifying their own poor behavior because they recognize, even if only subconsciously, that once they do, they will have to confront it.

### "Should you be doing that?"

*(Step 2 - His answer requires him to make a judgement call.)*

Often, simply asking someone if he thinks he should be doing the behavior helps him pause and consider.  He most often knows he shouldn't be doing what he's doing before you even ask.

Further, people often don't understand why they are doing what they are doing, or how to stop.  They haven't thought through their behavior well enough to figure that all out.  If they already know, they will usually reply, "No, I shouldn't be doing it."

However, they sometimes do not know they shouldn't be doing what they are doing.  This is because they have not had enough life experiences or instruction to think through the possible consequences of their behavior. They may reply, "Sure.  Why not?"  Now this is important!  <u>Resist the temptation to explain it to them</u> but move on to the next question.

And of course, there is the wise guy who answers "Yes" he thinks he should be doing it, or "Who cares, anyway?", or some other flippant answer.  If you persist and simply repeat your question, sincerely and repeatedly, they eventually admit that perhaps it isn't the best idea.  Try, "Do you really think this is a good idea?" repeated as needed.

**"What will happen if you do that?"**
*(Step 3 - He must be the one to identify possible consequences.)*
Here you have a choice.  If they have already said that they think they shouldn't be doing it, you can skip this question. If you think they are just saying it to get this over with you can pursue it a little more by repeating the question, perhaps in a slightly different form.  If they already know they are doing something that isn't going to help them in life, and you feel confident that they do you can skip to question four.

However, if they seem to truly not know that their behavior has consequences you can ask, "What will happen if (when) you do that?"  This forces them to think about possible scenarios that will likely stem from their behavior. It is often good too prompt deeper thought by asking, "What else?"

Sometimes they will give you simple reasons for not doing whatever they are doing.  Sometimes they may give silly reasons.  There is often grave resistance to thinking deeply about behavior.  You can help them dig deeper and be more thoughtful simply by asking, "Anything else?"  This can be repeated until you feel like a complete list of reasons why the behavior is inappropriate for reality has been given.

It is often hard to NOT suggest reasons to them why their behavior is harmful.  However, if you do that you will have identified the problem as yours.  You can, of course, suggest topics to explore.  "What affect do you think your behavior might have on your friendships?"  "Do you think your behavior might have any effects on your finances?"

**"Is that what you want to have happen?"**
*(Step 4 - He must make the value judgement about the consequences."*

Asking him if he wants those consequences will accomplish two things.  It will force him to make a value judgement about his behavior. He must personally tell you what he values. He may not even be aware of his own value system; this can be especially true for youth. However, even many adults are not entirely clear on their own value system.

But asking the person to make a judgement call about their consequences will tell you a lot about what they value. It doesn't matter that you understand this necessarily, but it will help you lead the discussion of plans in line with their own stated values. If one of the consequences is the loss of friendship, the student may say they don't care because they don't like those people anyway. This may or may not be true, but it does give insight about their values.

For example, he may not see getting sent to his room for lying as a very significant consequence.  If he shrugs his shoulders or acts unconcerned, you know that isn't a significant reason for him to change his behavior. Equally important, with this exchange he may begin to clarify and discover what his own set of values are.

At the same time, he may not have thought about the relationship between lying and trust, lying and friendship, or lying and the law.  He may only be thinking about how to get out of a tense situation without harm.  Once the reality of honesty, friendship and trust has been identified, he may see greater value in changing his behavior.

This discussion can be prolonged to deepen his understanding of why the behavior is harmful to him.  Often people will not have ever thoughtfully identified all the consequences of their behavior.  Reality begins when we understand our own value system and see clearly the possible results of our behavior on the things we value.

**"What can you do about it?"**
*(Step 5 - He makes his own plan or a series of steps to change behavior.)*
Asking him what they could do to avoid this behavior in the future allows him to begin formulating a plan.  It is

surprising how many people are not particularly good at making plans, especially long-reaching, change-of-life plans.

There may be multiple possibilities for changing what is happening in his life.  In fact, you may have already identified some things the person can do to make his life better.  However, they may not be things the person can do, or is willing to do.  Being an experienced problem solver does not mean that your problem solutions are the right ones for anyone else.  In fact, he might come up with solutions in his circumstance that you would never think of.

If the person is not particularly motivated or capable to come up with a plan, he will mutter some simple solution that may be half-hearted and unlikely to make a difference.  You can help at this point, not by telling them what to do but by asking something like, "Anything else?", or "What else could you do?" That will help them think through the process in a deeper and more realistic way.

Several alternatives might be developed, some of which you think are unlikely to make a difference.  However, continued questioning can help him focus on one good plan. That's when you move to the last question.

## "Will you do that?"

*Step 6 - He makes a verbal commitment to change his behavior.*

When you are satisfied that he has a plan, whether you think it is a good one or not, you simply ask him if he will do it.  Sometimes you might not think the plan is likely to succeed but remember that it is his plan.  Even if he fails, he will be more likely to explore other possibilities later, having tried his first plan already.

If he replies, "I'll try", or, "I'll see", or something similar, you know they are not committed.  It is important that they make the commitment out loud. It is easy to press them on this issue, just by teasingly stating that trying isn't doing, or by quoting Yoda from Star Wars.  "Do. Or do not. There is no try."

## How to use the questions

Obviously, sometimes this can be a very brief modified discussion. It could look as simple as this:

"What are you doing?"
>"Jumping on the bed."

"Should you be doing that?"
>"No."
>(Optional - What could happen if you jump on the bed?)

"What can you do about that?"
>"Stop."

"Will you?"
>"Yes."

On other occasions and concerning more complex behaviors, further probing and discussion may be required.  I think you will know when.

## In summary

Below are the six questions that will enable you to deal with misbehavior in a consistent, calm manner.  I have listed them separately from all the explanation to help you remember them and be able to focus on staying on each subject until it is answered fully.

1.  What are you doing?
2.  Should you be doing that?
3.  What will happen if you do that?
4.  Is that what you want to have happen?
5.  What can you do about it?
6.  Will you do that?

The advantages of this approach are that it is simple, consistent, effective, and allows one to remain calm and in control when dealing with misbehavior.  These are not trivial goals.

*"Reality can be beaten with enough imagination."*
*- Mark Twain -*

# EPILOGUE

*"Reality leaves a lot to the imagination."*
*- John Lennon -*

## What is real?

Humans are confused about language and frequently use terms in conflicting ways.  For example, people often dismiss an emotional experience as simply the physical events, not the feelings the events may have engendered. They may dismiss your feelings, on being threatened with violence, as, "All they did was holler at you.  You weren't really injured."

On the other hand, they often speak of reality as if it were the emotions caused by events.  "Well, it's fine for you to dismiss what happened as just hollering.  But you weren't there to see what it was really like to be threatened."

In one case they talk about reality as if it was only the actual physical, material facts.  In the other case they talk about reality as if it were the emotions and some mysterious force of the combined events.

One of the problems that has developed in our modern world is the philosophy that there is no such thing as truth.  It is common to hear people say things such as "Everything is relevant."  By this they mean that there is no truth, only what is true under current conditions.  It seems to escape those who hold this view that it is self-contradictory. If everything is relevant, then that statement is relevant, and something is true regardless of relevance. We do not claim to know the truth, but we think there is a truth that can be known and relied upon.

## Personal reality

When people talk about truth being relevant, I think they mean that there are personal situations and general considerations. However, we can know a great deal about how to live in our "real" world.  We know it already, at least as far as what our needs of the immediate future might be.

For example, in high school I simply could not fathom that someday I might need to understand some chemistry or world literature.  My mother had cancer, my older siblings had left home, my father was working night and day to support multiple families. I had several after school jobs, fixed my own meals and did my own laundry. Chemistry did not seem pertinent.

At the time I did not need to know the physics of falling bodies, how to predict a chemical reaction, how to solve a quadratic equation, or even that Hammurabi is credited with the first set of laws. The things I needed did not come from school, liberal arts, or science.  What I needed came from religion, philosophy, and negotiating my daily life.  I needed a job, so I could make some money.  I needed to fix my own lunches and wash my own clothes.  If I wanted to do something with friends, I needed a way to get to their house or the game.

Honestly, the knowledge that I probably needed most came from the so-called liberal arts, especially religion.  Do not lie, cheat, or steal.  Do not kill.  Do not be angry.  Do not covet.  Do not lust.  Eat and live wisely.  Avoid drugs, alcohol, and cigarettes. I suspect that, in daily life, reality is very different than the reality we talk about in the abstract. The "non-real" abstract subjects influence us at least as much moment-by-moment as the reality of the material world.

The liberal arts do not disdain facts or the reality of the material world.  In fact, they embrace it and use the material world in all kinds of non-material pursuits and activities. They use the material world to express non-material ideas and use non-material ideas to direct the material world.  Material concepts of electricity that underlie the internet can be used for good or ill purposes and are used in the service of abstract ideals.

In contrast, materialists often disdain the liberal arts as unimportant, imaginary, and frivolous.  This, while being subjected and responding to the very fields and activities they tend to treat as insignificant.  Their quest for objectivity, precision, and predictability in material blinds them to the significance and reality of the influence of the liberal arts.

Science might view everything out of this world as outer space.  But if there are other beings living in the universe, then we are outside of them.  If there is a God, then outer space is not outside of Him.  The term "outer-space" itself implies a provincial point of view and is just one example of human perception and hubris.

If we only see things from the liberal art point of view, we may react emotionally to matters that require physical and material solutions.  The humanist who decries the necessity of prisons has not considered the very real need for physical safety of society. Those who want free education, have not studied economics.

We live a little like goldfish in a bowl, unaware of the water changes and food raining down from above.  We pretend to be wise because we have discovered that food comes from above although we don't know the source.

## The significance of significance

Something can be both true and unimportant.  Not everyone seems to be able to make that distinction.  Of course, the meaning of importance may be as hard to come by as the meaning of the word true.  There are also things that are false that are important.  For example, there are important lies.  There are also things that are false but unimportant, and something can be true and important. However, we are faced with a dual prospect in life.  Not only must we determine what is true, we must determine which truths are important.

There are significant truths that effect our personal lives and humanity in significant ways.  For example, that we all must die is a significant truth.  It changes the value of time and time is what our life is made of.  The truths underlying the many beneficial uses, and occasional dangers, of electricity seem also to be significant.  There are many other examples.

Then there is what I will call isolated truth.  Isolated truth is much like isolated individuals.  Both exist without companionship or meaning.  Textbooks, and the internet, are filled with isolated truths.  These truths have little direct effect on our lives and may even seem to exist without any connection to anything else.  John Silber, one-time President of Boston University, once observed: "One can forget the meaninglessness of his own existence by occupying himself with scientific experiments of dubious import."

One can do the same by writing music of no lasting distinction, writing hack novels, painting pictures for no purpose, or pursuing money for self-gratification.  Isolated facts, and people, wander in search of companionship and meaning.

Worse than isolated truths are useless and irrelevant truths.  These things may have been true but are no longer, like the bus schedule from 1992 or my military service number from 1966.  It is still true, and I still know it. I don't know why.

There are things that are true in one place that are not true in other places or situations such as the price of a gallon of gas in various countries.   And there are things that are true, but which do not affect us in any significant way.  The opinions of celebrities on just about anything.

There are things that are true and not relative.  And some truths are simply more important than others, over time, place, and circumstance.  Things that are ultimately true do not change over distance or time.  If something is true in Africa it is true in Canada.  If something is true in 1556 it is true today and will be true in a hundred years.

It is as important to determine between which truths are most important as to distinguish between fact and fancy.  Thus, we are faced with a dual problem; determining truth and assigning importance or priority.

### What is important?

Determining what is true is easier than determining what is important.  It may take a lot of time and effort, but one can usually come to some understanding about what is true, even in politics.  It is a general rule that we never have enough information for a final determination of truth.  But we can often come to a good and accurate decision if we are willing to put forth the effort to gather data and think clearly.

However, what is important seems to be a moving target. Under one set of conditions just staying alive may be the most important thing you can apply yourself to.  Under a different set of conditions risking death may seem worth the risk.  In some situations, killing mosquitoes may be the most important thing you can do. In a different circumstance raising bees may seem more pressing.

If we are doing something important, we probably want to know if we are making progress.  Progress just sounds like something one should want to do.  However, progress can only make sense when there is a sure goal.  If the goal keeps changing, shifting further out, or changing directions, one is no longer making progress towards achieving anything.  They are now just moving around.

In contrast to truth, something can be "important" in 1556 but not today, or something can be "important" in Africa but not in Canada.  Some truths are simply more universal and "important" than others over time and distance. Truth and reality are the same thing. There are insignificant facts of reality and significant facts of reality. Reality is not relevant just as truth is not relevant. It is important that children especially, and some adults, learn to correctly identify and live in reality

## Why we wrote this book

The reason for writing this book is to provide a method of helping children learn to conduct themselves in a way that is compatible with reality.  Fortunately, the same methods can also be useful in helping some adults with behavior problems. Many people of all ages who misbehave in some way have never learned how to live peacefully with reality. Accepting reality can have a great effect on helping people change and find greater happiness and success in life.

"What we achieve inwardly will
change outer reality."
- Plutarch -

## ABOUT THE AUTHORS

Gary and Gaydra McCallister are life-long teachers and the parents of four grown children.  Gary has a doctorate in biological science and taught at the University level for over forty years.  Gaydra has a master's degree in Science education and taught elementary school for twenty years.  The rest of the time she was full time Mom.  They are now participating grandparents to eighteen grandchildren.  Helping others with poor and self-destructive behavior is the only career they have known.  So far as is known, none of their students or own children have died or been injured because of facing REALITY.

*OTHER BOOKS BY GARY MCCALLISTER*

*MUSIC*
*Making More than Music 2014*
*First Songs with the Mountain Dulcimer: history, instrument, and simple songs 2015*
*Hymns on Mountain Dulcimer: Learn to play the mountain dulcimer using hymns 2016*

*SCIENCE*
*Hanging Out With GRAVITY: Galileo's gravity game 2015*

*Seriously Silly Science: A science reader for the whole year - and some of it is even true 2015*

*A Convenient Truce: A cease fire in the war between religion and science 2016*

*The Solar Solution: the solution to problems you didn't even know you had. 2017*

*Thou Shalt Make: the spiritual significance of making things. 2019.*

*HISTORY*
*The Hammar's of History by Harold and Jerry Hammar*
*GM - Compiler, editor, and publisher*

*NOVELS*
*Walking Man 2015*

*All available on Amazon.com*

www.ingramcontent.com/pod-product-compliance
Lightning Source LLC
Chambersburg PA
CBHW050759240726

48654CB00008B/553